AF405752

# The God who Answers Prayer

The God who Answers Prayer
Copyright © 2023 by Vincent A. Piccone, M.D.

Published in the United States of America
ISBN   Paperback:      979-8-89091-011-0
ISBN   eBook:           979-8-89091-012-7

All rights reserved. No part of this publication may be reproduced, stored in a retrieval system or transmitted in any way by any means, electronic, mechanical, photocopy, recording or otherwise without the prior permission of the author except as provided by USA copyright law.

The opinions expressed by the author are not necessarily those of ReadersMagnet, LLC.

ReadersMagnet, LLC
10620 Treena Street, Suite 230
San Diego, California, 92131 USA
1.619. 354. 2643 | www.readersmagnet.com

Book design copyright © 2023 by ReadersMagnet, LLC. All rights reserved.

Cover design by Ericka Obando
Interior design by Don De Guzman

# The God who Answers Prayer

Vincent A. Piccone, M.D.

# Introduction

The God of the Universe, the God who created you, me and everything else that is in the world gave us a way to communicate with him. This communication is called prayer. Whether it be a recital of our deepest yearnings and aspirations or a simple thank you for everything that God does for us-God hears our prayers. Some people pray on their knees and some people pray while lying on their beds.

In this book the author has referenced those bible verses that include the word prayer and has tried to explain their use in the context of God's word. The author has also included the prayers of important people mentioned in the bible to illustrate examples of how men have prayed in the past.

The word "PRAY" gives us a formula for how we should pray to God. "P" can stand for "praise" in which we give glory to God for his awesomeness and majesty and for all he has done for us. "R" can stand for the word repent in which we ask forgiveness for our sins. "A" can stand for ask in which we request of God those things we think we need. "Y" can stand for yield in which we stand back and let God into our lives so that he can direct us and guide us in a way best for our particular life's situation.

God always hears prayer though he doesn't always answrs prayers. Sometimes he says yes to our requests; Sometimes he says no; and sometimes he says maybe or not now. There is a saying watch for what your pray for because you might get it. We must be respectful, humble, and careful what we pray for.

God will not hear prayer on occasion. When we prayer to someone else's detriment, to our own harm, or out of selfishness God often rejects our prayers. One bible verse reads "To one who does not keep the law, even his prayer is an abomination." God delights in hearing and answering the prayers of the faithful and to those who keep his commandments.

# The Lord's Prayer

**"This is how you are to pray:
Our Father in Heaven, hallowed be your name,
Your kingdom come, your will be done,
on earth as in heaven. Give us
today our daily bread;
and forgive us our debts, as we forgive
our debtors; and do not subject us to
the final test, but deliver us from the evil one."**

**Matthew 6:9-13**

Jesus taught us how to pray. We are to recite the above prayer every day of our lives. The prayer makes holy the name of God. It asks that we by our words and actions we further God's kingdom on earth and make life on earth more heavenlike. It asks of God that we receive sustenance for our bodies and souls on daily basis. It asks for the strength to forgive people who sin against us and that God forgive our sins against him and against our neighbor. The LORD's prayer asks that we be not led into temptation but protected from evil.

"He was praying in a certain place, and when he had finished, one of his disciples said to him, "Lord, teach us to pray just a John taught his disciples." He said to them, "When you pray, say: Father hallowed be your name, your kingdom come. Give us each day our daily bread and forgive us our sins for we ourselves forgive everyone in debt to us and do not subject us to the final test."

Luke 11:1-4.

Luke's version of the Lord's prayer is shorter than Matthew's but has essentially the same content. Matthew's version of the prayer is probably the more prayed prayer.

# Prayer-Why Pray?

He rescued us from such great danger of death, and he will continue to rescue us; in him we have put our hope that he will also rescue us again, as you help us with prayer, so that thanks may be given by many on our behalf for the gift granted us through the prayers of many.

2 Corinthians 1:10-11

For everything created by God is good, and nothing is to be rejected with thanksgiving, for it is made holy by the invocation of God in prayer.

1 Timothy 4:4-5

What is the Almighty that we should serve him? And what do we gain by praying to him?

Job 21:1

Forgive your neighbor the wrong done to you;
Then when you pray, your own sins will be forgiven.
Sirach 28:2

After all the people had been baptized and Jesus had been baptized and was praying, heaven was opened and the holy Spirit descended upon him in bodily form like a dove. And a voice came from heaven, "You are my beloved Son; with you I am well pleased."
Luke 3:21-22

When you pray, when you talk with God, when you communicate with God-You acknowledge God as your creator, your sustenance, and your deliverer. Why pray?-because it is the most important thing you do all day. Prayer brings us close to God. Who knows? When we pray, one day the sky might open up and a voice be heard "You are my beloved child". What do we gain by praying to God? In praying we put ourselves in God's hands. Our fate is linked with God's plans for our lives and he wants only the very best for us. When we pray our anxiety dissolves and our legs become girded. Prayer leads to holiness in our lives. When we pray God rescues us from temptation and evil. When we ask for in prayer, God often delivers. Prayer puts our lives into perspective and crystalizes our relationship with God. Prayer humbles us and allows us to know how much we really need God.

# Prayer-Prayer God does not hear

You wrapped yourself in wrath and pursued us, killing without pity. You wrapped yourself in a cloud, which no prayer could pierce.

Lamentations 3:43-44

When we rebel against God and are obstinate, and he has not forgiven us then God does not hear our prayer. When we anger God by our words and actions he does not hear our prayer even if is to ask God to save us.

He has hemmed me in with no escape, weighed me down with chains; Even when I cry for help, he stops my prayer.

Lamentations 3:7-7

The book of lamentations is full of God's punishment for the people's sins. The punishment is accompanied by God's failure to hear prayer. If we live in a sinful state or have sinned grievously against God he will not hear our prayer.

Do not babble in the assembly of the elders or repeat the words of your prayer.

Sirach 7-14

Repetition of prayers in public or before others has the effect of cancelling our prayers to God. God asks us to pray to him in private. Our prayers should not be babble but well thought out requests to God.

In praying, do not babble like the pagans, who think they will be heard because of their many words. Do not be like them. Your Father knows what you need before you ask him.

Matthew 6:7-8

The full quote is "When you pray, do not be like the hypocrites, who love to stand and pray in the synagogues and on street corners so that others may see them. Amen, I say to you, they have received their reward. But when you pray, go to your inner room, close the door, and pray to your Father in secret. And your Father who sees in secret will repay you. These statements would indicate that God wants us to communicate directly with him in private. These are the prayers God hears; not those we offer in public.

LORD of hosts, how long will you smolder in anger while your people pray?

Psalm 80:5

This verse in the psalm is followed with "LORD of hosts, how long will you burn with anger while your people pray? You have fed them the bread of tears, made them drink tears in abundance. You have left us to be fought over by our neighbors; our enemies deride us.

But when he prays about his goods or marriage or children, he is not ashamed to address the thing without a soul.

Wisdom 13:17

The above verse pertains to idolatry. If people pray to idols in violation of the first commandment-though shall not take false Gods before you-then God abandons us to the idols and absolutely will not hear our prayer. The same applies to the idols of money, wealth, and power. When we worship these idols God rejects our prayers. God hears our prayers when we worship and obey him.

# Pray All the Time

"Persevere in prayer, being watchful in it with thanksgiving; at the same time, pray for us, too, that God may open a door to us for the word, to speak of the mystery of Christ, for which I am in prison, that I may make it clear, as I must speak."

Collosians4:2-4

"Pray without ceasing."

1 Thessalonians 5:17

"With all prayer and supplication, pray for every opportunity in the spirit."

Ephesians 6-18

"Rejoice in hope, endure in affliction, persevere in prayer."

Romans 12:12

"Then he told them a parable about the necessity for them to pray always without becoming weary. He said, "there was a judge in a certain town who neither feared God nor respected any human being. And a widow in that town used to come to him and say, ' render a just decision for me against my adversary.' For a long time the judge was unwilling, but eventually he thought, ' while it is true that I neither fear God nor respect any human being, because this widow keeps bothering me I shall deliver a just decision for her lest she finally come and strike me' "The Lord said, "Pay attention to what the dishonest judge says. Will not God then secure the rights of his chosen ones who call out to him day and night? Will he be slow to answer them? I tell you, he will see to it that justice is done for them speedily. But when the Son of Man comes, will he find faith on earth."

Matthew 18:1-8

The Lion's Den. Darius decided to appoint over his entire kingdom one hundred and twenty satraps. These were accountable to three ministers, one of whom was Daniel; the satraps reported to them, so that the king should suffer no loss. Daniel outshone all the ministers and satraps because an extraordinary spirit was in him, and the king considered setting him over the entire kingdom. Then the ministers and satraps tried to find grounds for accusation against Daniel regarding the kingdom. But they could not accuse him of any corruption. Because he was trustworthy, no fault or corruption was to be found in him. Then these men said to themselves, "We shall find no grounds for accusation against this Daniel except in connection with the law of his God." So these ministers and satraps stormed in to the king and said to him "King Darius, live forever! All the ministers of the kingdom, the prefects, satraps, counselors, and governors agree that the following prohibition ought to be put in force by royal decree: no one is to address any petition to god or man for thirty days, except to you, O king; otherwise he shall be cast into a den of lions. Now, O king, issue the prohibition over your signature, immutable and irrevocable under Mede and Persian law." So king Darius signed the prohibition and made it law.

Even after Daniel heard that this law had been signed, he continued his custom of going home to knell in prayer and give thanks to his God in the upper chamber three times a day, with the windows open toward Jerusalem. So these men rushed in an found Daniel praying and pleading before his God. Then they went to remind the king about the prohibition: "Did you not decree, O king, that no one is to address a petition to god or man for thirty days, except to you, O King; otherwise he shall be cast into a den of lions?" The king answered them, "The decree is absolute, irrevocable under the Mede and Persian law." To this day they replied, "Daniel, the Jewish exile, has paid no attention to you, O king, or the decree you issued; three times a day, he offers his prayer." The king was deeply grieved at this news and he made up his mind to save Daniel; he worked till sunset to rescue him. But these men insisted, "Keep in mind, O king,", they said that under the Mede and Persian law every royal prohibition or decree is irrevocable." So the king ordered Daniel to be brought and cast into the lion's den. To Daniel he said, "May your God, whom you serve so constantly, save you." To forestall any tampering, the king sealed with his own ring and the rings of the lords the stone that had been brought to block the opening of the den.

Then the king returned to his palace for the night; he refused to eat and he dismissed the entertainers. Since sleep was impossible for him, the king rose very early the next morning and hastened to the lion's den. As he drew near, he cried out to Daniel sorrowfully, "O Daniel, servant of the living God, has the God whom you serve so constantly been able to save you from the lions?" Daniel answered the king: "O king, live forever! My God has sent his angels and closed the lion's mouths so that they have not hurt me. For I have been found innocent before him; neither to you have I done any harm, O king!" This gave the king great joy. At his order Daniel was removed from the den, unhurt because he trusted in his God. The king then ordered the men who had accused Daniel, along with their children and their wives, to be cast into the lion's den. Before they reached the bottom of the den, the lions overpowered them and crushed all their bones.

Then king Darius wrote to the nations an peoples of every language, wherever they dwell on the earth:" All peace to you! I decree that throughout my royal domain the God of Daniel is to be reverenced and feared: "For he is the living God, enduring forever; his kingdom shall not be destroyed, and his dominion shall be without end. He is a deliverer and savior, working signs and wonders in heaven and on earth, and he delivered Daniel from the lions' power."

Daniel 6:2-28

The above passages illustrate the frequency with which we are to pray. The "our father" prayer should be said daily and indeed the bible quotes suggest we should pray often if not continuously during the day. Daniel kneeled in prayer three times a day. All in all we should consciously pray every day of our lives. If we can we should pray as often as we can during the day. When we pray often it keeps God's eye on us and keeps us in his thoughts. Frequent prayer focuses our minds on what he hold important and gives us guidance too for what we should consider important.

# Pray-Where to Pray

Then he made his disciples get into the boat and precede him to the other side toward Bethsaida, while he dismissed the crown. And when he had taken leave of them, he went off to the mountain to pray.

Mark 6:45-46

Then he made the disciples get into the boat and precede him to the other side, while he dismissed the crowds. After doing so, he went up on the mountain by himself to pray. When it was evening he was there alone.

Matthew 14:22-23

On the Sabbath we went outside the city gate along the river where we thought there would be a place of prayer. We sat and spoke with the women who had gathered there.

Acts 16:13

When you pray, do not be like the hypocrites, who love to stand and pray in the synagogues and on street corners so that others may see them. Amen I say to you, they have received their reward. But when you pray, go to your inner room, close the door, and pray to your Father in secret. And your Father who sees in secret will repay you.

Matthew 6:5-6

There was also a prophetess, Anna, the daughter of Phanuel, of the tribe of Ascher. She was advanced in years, having lived seven years with her husband after her marriage, and then as a widow until she was eighty-four. She never left the temple, but worshipped night and day with fasting and prayer.

Luke 3:36-37


Then they assembled and went to Mizpah near Jerusalem, because formerly at Mizpah there was a place of prayer for Israel.

1 Maccabees 3:46


When we are young we are taught by our parents to kneel by the side of our bed and pray before sleep. Prayer, however, can be anywhere any time. Church or synagogue is a good place to pray on our knees. The best place for us to pray is in our inner room of our house where our Father who sees in secret will repay us. There are other bible verses that make it clear we can pray anywhere. Jesus prayed on the mountains and the Garden of Gethsemane. Daniel prayed on his knees but any position whether standing or lying down on our beds is acceptable.

## Prayer of Hannah

Hannah rose after one such meal at Shiloh, and presented herself before the LORD; at the time, Eli the priest was sitting on a chair near the doorpost of the LORD's temple. In her bitterness she prayed to the LORD, weeping copiously, and she made a vow promising: O LORD of hosts, if you look with pity on the misery of your handmaid, if you remember me and do not forget me, if you give your handmaid a male child, I will give him to the LORD for as long as he lives; neither wine nor liquor shall he drink, and no razor shall ever touch his head." As she remained long at prayer before the LORD< Eli watched her mouth, for Hannah was praying silently; though her lips were moving, her voice could not be heard.

1 Samuel 1:9-13

Hannah, the wife of Elkanah had no children and was ridiculed by Peninnah, Elkanah's other wife. Hannah in her bitterness prays for a child. Her prayer is heard.

# David's Prayer

Then David blessed the LORD in the presence of the whole assembly, praying in these words: "Blessed may you be, O LORD, God of Israel our father, from eternity to eternity. Yours, O LORD, are grandeur and power, majesty, splendor, and glory. For all in heaven and on earth is yours; yours, O LORD is the sovereignty; you are exalted as head over all. "Riches and honor are from you, and you have dominion over all. In your hand are power and might; it is yours to give grandeur and strength to all. Therefore, our God, we give you thanks and we praise the majesty of your name." "But who am I, and who are my people, that we should have the means to contribute so freely? For everything is from you, and we only give what we have received from you. For we stand before you as aliens; we are only your guests, like all our fathers. Our life on earth is only a shadow that does not abide. O LORD our God, all this wealth that we have brought together to build you a house in honor of your holy name comes from you and is entirely yours. I know, O my God, that you put hearts to the test and you take pleasure in uprightness. With a sincere heart I have willingly given all these things, and now with joy I have seen your people here present also giving to you generously. O LORD, God of our fathers Abraham,

Isaac, and Israel, keep such thoughts in the hearts and minds forever, and direct their hearts toward you. Give to my son Solomon a wholehearted desire to keep your commandments, precepts and statutes, that he may carry out all these plans and build the castle for which I have made preparation."

1 Chronicles 29:10-19

David worships God for his greatness and majesty. David acknowledges that all the people offer God comes from God. David asks God to have his son Solomon serve God faithfully. God hears and answers David's prayer.

# Hezekiah's Prayer

Hezekiah took the letter from the hand of the messengers and read it; he then went up to the temple of the LORD, and spreading it out before him, he prayed in the LORD's presence: "O LORD, God of Israel, enthroned upon the cherubim! You alone are God over all the kingdoms of the earth. You have made the heavens and the earth. Incline your eyes, O LORD and see! Hear the words of Sennacherib which he sent to taunt the living God. Truly, O LORD, the kings of Assyria have laid waste the nations and their lands, and cast their gods into the fire; they destroyed them because they were not gods, but the work of human hands, wood and stone. Therefore, O LORD, our God, save us from the power of this man, that all the kingdoms of the earth may know that you alone, o LORD, are God.

2Kings 19:14-19

The Assyrian army was to conquer Israel. Hezekiah relied on the LORD to protect the Israelites from the Assyrians. Hezekiah prayed that God save them from the Assyrians and that the people might know that the LORD os God alone. His prayer is heard and answered.

# Prayers of Tobiah, Tobit and Sarah
# Tobit

## Tobit's Prayer for Death

Grief-stricken in spirit, I groaned and wept aloud. Then with sobs I began to pray: "You are righteous, O LORD, and all your deeds are just; All your ways are mercy and truth; you are the judge of the world. And now, O LORD, may you be mindful of me, and look with favor upon me. Punish me not for my sins, nor for my inadvertent offenses, nor for those of my fathers. "They sinned against you, and disobeyed your commandments. So you handed us over to plundering, exile, and death, till we were and object lesson, a byword, a reproach in all the nations among whom you scattered us. "Yes, your judgments are many and true in dealing with me as my sins and those of my fathers deserve. For we have notkept your commandments, nor have we trodden the paths of truth before you. "So now, deal with me as you please, and command my life breath to be taken from me, that I may from the face of the earth into dust. It is better for me to die than to live, because I have heard insulting calumnies, and I am overwhelmed with grief. " Lord, command me to be delivered from such anguish; let me go to the everlasting abode; Lord, refuse me not. For it is better for me to die than to endure so much misery in life, and to hear these insults!"

Tobit 3:1-6

# Sarah's Prayer for Death

At that time, then she spread out her hands, and facing the window, poured out this prayer: "Blessed are you, O Lord merciful God! Forever blessed and honored is your holy name; may all your works forever bless you. And now, O Lord, to you I turn my face and raise my eyes. Bid me to depart from the earth, never again to hear such insults. "You know, O Master, that I am innocent of any impure act with a man, And that I have never defiled my own name or my father's name in the land of my exile. "I am my father's only daughter, and he has no other child to make his heir, Nor does he have a close kinsman or other relative whom I might bide my time to marry. I have already lost seven husbands; why then should I live any longer? But if it please you, Lord, not to slay me, look favorable upon me and have pity on me; never again let me hear these insults!"

Tobit 3:11-15

At that very time, the prayer of these two suppliants was heard in the presence of Almighty God. So Raphael was sent to heal them both: to remove the cataract's from Tobits eyes, so that he might again see God's sunlight; and to marry Raguel's daughter Sarah to Tobit's son Tobiah, and then drive the wicked demon Asmodeus from her.

Tobit 3:16-17

# Prayer of Tobiah

When the girl's parents left the bedroom and closed the door behind them, Tobiah arose from bed and said to his wife, "My love, get up. Let us pray and beg our Lord to have mercy on us and to grant us deliverance." She got up, and they started to pray that deliverance might be theirs. He began with these words: "Blessed are you, O God of our fathers; praised be your name forever and ever. Let the heavens and all your creation praise you forever. You made Adam and gave him his wife Eve to be is help and support; and from these two the human race descended. You said, "It is not good for the man to be alone let us make him a partner like himself.' Now, Lord, you know that I take this wife of mine not because of lust but for a noble purpose. Call down your mercy on me and on her, and allow us to live together to a happy old age."

Tobit 8:4-7

I can now tell you that when you, Tobit, and Sarah prayer, it was I who presented and read the record of your prayer before the Glory of the Lord.

Tobit 12:12 -13

Then Tobit composed this joyful prayer: Blessed be God who lives forever, because his kingdom lasts for all ages. For he scourges and then has mercy; he casts down to the depths of the netherworld, and he brings up from the great abyss. No one can escape his hand. Praise him, you Israelites, before the Gentiles, for though he has scattered you among them, he has shown you his greatness even there. Exalt him before every living being, because he is the Lord our God, our Father and God forever. He scourged you for your iniquities, but will again have mercy on you all. He will gather you from all the Gentiles among whom you have been scattered. When you turn back to him with all your heart, to do what is right before him, Then he will turn back to you, and no longer hide his face from you. So now consider what he has done for you, and praise him with full voice. Bless the Lord of righteousness, and exalt the King of the ages. In the Land of my exile I praise him, and show his power and majesty to a sinful nation. "Turn back you sinners! Do the right before him: perhaps he may look with favor upon you and show you mercy. "As for me, I exalt my God, and my spirit rejoices in the King of heaven. Let all men speak of his majesty, and sing his praises in Jerusalem." O Jerusalem, holy city, be scourged for the work of your hands, but will again pity the children of the righteous. Praise the Lord for his goodness, and bless the King of the ages, so that his tent may be rebuilt in you with joy. May he gladded within you all who were captives; all who were ravaged may he cherish within you for all generations to come. A bright light will shine on all parts of the earth; many nations shall come to you from afar, And the inhabitants of all the limits of the earth, drawn to you by the name of the Lord God, Bearing in their hands their gifts for the King of heaven. Every generation shall give joyful praise in you, and shall call you the chosen one, through all ages forever. Accursed are all who speak a harsh word against you; accursed are all who destroy you and pull down your walls, And all who overthrow your towers and set fire to your homes; but forever blessed are all those who build you up. Go, then rejoice over the children of the righteous, who shall be gathered together and shall bless the Lord of the ages. Happy are those who love you, and happy those who rejoice in your prosperity. Happy are all the men who grieve over you, over all your chastisements, For they shall rejoice in you as they rejoice in you as they behold all your joy forever. My spirit blesses the Lord, the great king; Jerusalem shall be rebuilt as his home forever. Happy for me if a remnant of my offspring survive to see your glory and to praise the King of heaven! The gates of Jerusalem shall be built with sapphire and emerald, and all your walls with precious stones. The towers of Jerusalem shall be built with gold, and their battlements with pure gold. The streets of Jerusalem shall be paved with rubies and stones of Ophir; The gates of Jerusalem shall sing hymns of gladness, and all their houses shall cry out, "alleluia!" "Blessed be God who has raised you up! May he be blessed for all ages!" For in you they shall praise his holy name forever.

Tobit 13:1-18

Tobit is blind an miserable. He prays for death. Sarah has lost seven husbands and is msierable. She also prays for death. God hears the prayers of these two people and brings abouut a very happy ending. Tobit regains his sight and Tobiah, Tobits son marries Sarah to bring them both great happiness.

# The Prayer of Azariah

They walked about in the flames, singing to God and blessing the Lord. Azariah stood up in the midst of the fire and prayed aloud:

"Blessed are you, and praiseworthy, O Lord, the God of our ancestors, and glorious forever is your name. For you are just in all you have done; and your deeds are faultless, all your ways right, and your judgements proper. You have executed proper judgements in all that you have brought upon us and upon Jerusalem, the holy city of our ancestors. By a proper judgement you have done all this because of our sins; For we have sinned and transgressed by departing from you, and we have done every kind of evil. Your commandments we have not heeded or observed, nor have we done as you ordered for us for our good. Therefore all you have brought upon us, all that you have done to us, you have done by a proper judgement. You have handed us over to our enemies, lawless and hateful rebels; to an unjust king, the worst in all the world. Now we cannot open our mouths; shame and reproach have come upon us, your servants who revere you. For your name's sake, do not deliver us up forever, or make void your covenant. Do not take your mercy from us, for the sake of Abraham, your beloved, Isaac your servant, and Israel your holy one, To whom you promised to multiply their offspring like the stars of heaven, or the sand on the shore of the sea. For we are reduced, O Lord, beyond any other nation, brought low everywhere in the world this day because of our sins. We have in our day no prince, prophet, or leader, no burnt offering, sacrifice, oblation, or incense, no place to offer first fruits, to find favor with you. But with contrite heart and humble spirit let us be received; As though it were holocausts of rams and bullocks, or thousands of fat lambs. So let our sacrifice be in your presence today as we follow you unreservedly for those who trust in you cannot be put to shame. And now we follow you with our whole heart, we fear you and pray to you. Do not let us be put to shame, but deal with us in your kindness and great mercy. Deliver us by your wonders, and bring us to your name, O Lord: Let all those be routed who inflict evils on your servants; Let them be shamed and powerless, and their strength broken; Let them know that you alone are the Lord God, glorious over the whole world."

Daniel 3:26-45

The Jewish exiles who were made high officials under Nebuchadnezzar, the king, refuse to worship the golden statue-god set up by Nebuchadnezzar. The Jews were thrown into a fiery furnace. Miraculously, they are untouched by the fire. Azariah prays out loud in the fire. Azariah confesses the sins of the people and asks forgiveness and protection from the flames.

# Prayers of Nehimiah

I asked them about the Jews, the remnant preserved after the captivity, and about Jerusalem, and they answered me: "The survivors of the captivity there in the province are in great distress and under reproach. Also the wall of Jerusalem lies breached, and its gates have been gutted with fire." When I heard this report, I began to weep and continued morning for several days; I fasted and prayed before the God of heaven.

I prayed: "O LORD, God of heaven, great and awesome God, you who preserve your covenant of mercy toward those who love you and keep your commandments, may your ear be attentive, and your eyes open, to heed they prayer which I your servant, now offer in your presence day and night for your servants the Israelites, confessing the sins which we of Israel have committed against you, I and my father's house included. Grievously have we offended you, not keeping the commandments, the statutes, and the ordinances which you committed to your servant Moses. But remember, I pray, the promise which you gave through Moses, your servant, when you said: ' Should you prove faithless, I will scatter you among the nations; but should you return to me and carefully keep my commandments, even though your outcasts have been driven to the farthest corner of the world, I will gather them from there, and bring them back to the place which I have chosen as the dwelling place for my name.' They are your servants, your people, whom you freed by your great might and your strong hand. O LORD, may your ear be attentive to my prayer and that of all your willing servants who revere your name. Grant success to you servant this day, and let him find favor with this man"---for I was cupbearer to the king.

Nehemiah 1:2-11

The king asked me, "What is it, then, that you wish?"" I prayed to the God of heaven, and then answered the king: "If it please the king, and if your servant is deserving of your favor, send me to Judah, to the city of my ancestors' graves to rebuild it."

Nehemiah 2:4-5

Thereupon they all plotted together to come and fight against Jerusalem and thus to throw us into confusion. We prayed to our God and posted a watch against them day and night for fear of what they might do.

Nehemiah 4:2-3

# Prayer-Of Jonathan and Nehemiah

While the sacrifice was being burned, the priests recited a prayer, and all present joined in with them, Jonathan leading and the rest responding with Nehemiah. The prayer was as follows: "LORD, LORD God, creator of all things, awesome and strong, just and merciful, the only king and benefactor, who alone are gracious, just almighty, and eternal, Israel's savior from all evil, who chose our forefathers and sanctified them: accept this sacrifice on behalf of all your people Israel and guard and sanctify your heritage. Gather together our scattered people, free those who are the slaves of the gentiles, look kindly on those who are despised and detested, and let the Gentiles know that you are our God. Punish those who tyrannize over us and arrogantly mistreat us. Plant your people in your holy place, as Moses promised."

2 Maccabees 2:24-29

# Solomon's Prayer

Solomon then took his place before the altar of the Lord in the presence of the whole community of Israel and stretched forth his hands. He had made a bronze platform five cubits long, five cubits wide, and five cubits high, which he had placed in the center of the courtyard. Having ascended it, Solomon knelt in the presence of the whole of Israel and stretched forth his hands toward heaven…. Thus he prayed: "LORD, God of Israeli, there is no God like you in heaven or on earth: you keep your covenant and show kindness to your servants who are wholeheartedly faithful to you. You have kept the promise you made to my father David, your servant. With your own mouth you spoke it, and by your own hand you have brought it to fulfillment this day. Now, therefore, LORD, God of Israel, keep the further promise you made to my father David, your servant, when you said, 'You shall always have someone from your line to sit before me on the throne of Israel, provided only that your descendants look to their conduct so as to always live according to my law, even as you have lived in my presence.' Now, LORD, God of Israel, may this promise which you made to your servant David be confirmed.

"Can it indeed be that God dwells with mankind on earth? If the heavens and the highest heavens cannot contain you, how much less this temple which I have built! Look kindly on the prayer and petition of your of your servant, O LORD, my God, and listen to the cry of supplication your servant makes before you. May your eyes watch day and night over this temple, the place where you have decreed you shall be honored; may you heed the prayer which I your servant offer toward this place. Listen to the petitions of your servant and of your people Israel, which they direct toward this place. Listen from your heavenly dwelling, and when you have heard, pardon.

When any man sins against his neighbor and is required to take on oath of execration against himself, and when he comes for the oath before your altar in this temple, listen from heaven: take action and pass judgement on your servants, requiting the wicked man and holding him responsible for his conduct, but absolving the innocent and rewarding him according to his virtue. When your people Israel have sinned against you and are defeated by the enemy, but afterward they return and praise your name, and they pray to you and entreat you in this temple, listen from heaven and forgive the sin of your people Israel, and bring them back to the land which you gave them and their fathers. When the sky is closed so that there is no rain, because they have sinned against you, but then they pray toward this place and praise your name, and they withdraw from sin because you afflict them, listen in heaven and forgive the sin of your servant and your people Israel. But teach them the right way to live, and send rain upon your land which you gave their people as their heritage. When there is famine in the land, when there is pestilence, or blight, or mildew, or locusts, or caterpillars; when their enemies besiege them at any on their gate; whenever there is a plague or sickness of any kind; when any Israelite of all your people offers a payer or petition of any kind, and in awareness of his affliction and pain, stretches out his hands towards toward this temple, listen from your heavenly dwelling place and forgive. Knowing his heart, render to everyone according tohis conduct, for you alone known the hearts of men. So may they fear you and walk in your ways as long as they live on the land you gave our fathers.

For the foreigner, too, who is not of your people Israel, when he comes from a distant land to honor your great name, your mighty power, and your outstretched arm, when they come in prayer to this temple, listen from your heavenly dwelling place, and do whatever the foreigner entreats you, that all the peoples of the earth may know your name, fearing you as do your people Israel, and knowing that this house which I have built is dedicated to your honor.

When your people go forth to war against their enemies, wherever you send them, and pray to you in the direction of this city and the house I have built in your honor, listen from heaven to their prayer and petition, and defend their cause. When they sin against you (for there is no man who does not sin), and in your anger against them you deliver them to the enemy, so that their captors deport them to another land, far or near, when they repent in the land where they are captive and are converted, when they entreat you in the land of their captivity and say, 'We have sinned and done wrong; we have been wicked,' and with their whole heart and with their while soul they turn back to you in the land of those who hold them captive, when they pray in the direction of their land which you gave their fathers, and of the city which you have chose, and of the house which I built to your honor, listen from your heavenly dwelling place, hear their prayers and petitions, and uphold their cause. Forgive your people who have sinned against you. My God, may your eyes be open and your ears attentive to the prayer of this place. And now, "Advance, LORD God to your resting place, you and the ark of your majesty. May your priests, LORD God, be clothed with salvation, may your faithful ones rejoice in good things. LORD God, reject not the plea of your anointed, remember the devotion of David, your servant."

When Solomon had ended his prayer, fire came down from heaven and consumed the holocaust and the sacrifices, and the glory of the LORD filled the house.

2 Chronicles 6:12-7:1

Solomon prays for the people and for the temple he built to the LORD. He asks that the wicked be condemned and that the just be acquitted. He prays that the people repent of their sins and ask forgiveness, that God give then rain in drought, food in famine, and victory against enemies.

Solomon stood before the altar of the LORD in the presence of the whole community of Israel, and stretching forth his hands toward heaven, he said "LORD, God of Israel, there is no God like you in heaven above or on earth below; you keep your covenant of kindness with your servants who are faithful to you with their whole heart. You have kept the promise you made to my father David, your servant. You who spoke that promise, have this day, by your own power, brought it to fulfillment. Now, therefore, LORD. God of Israel, keep the further promise you made to my father David, your servant, saying, 'You shall always have someone from your line to sit before me on the throne of Israel, provided only that your descendants look to their conduct so that they live in my presence, as you have lived in my presence.' Now, LORD, God of Israel, may this promise that you made to my father David, your servant be confirmed.

"Can it indeed be that God dwells among men on earth? If the heavens and the highest heavens cannot contain you, how much less this temple which I have built! Look kindly on the prayer and petition of your servant, O LORD, my God, and listen to the cry of supplication which I, your servant, utter before you this day. May your eyes watch day and night over this temple, the place where you have decreed you shall be honored; may you heed the prayer which I, your servant, offer in this place Listen to the petitions of your servant and your people Israel which they offer in this place. Listen from your heavenly dwelling and grant pardon.

"If a man sins against his neighbor and is required to take an oath sanctioned by a curse, when he comes and takes an oath before your altar in this temple, listen in heaven; take action and pass judgement on your servants. Condemn the wicked and punish him for his conduct, but acquit the just and establish his innocence.

"If your people Israel sin against you and are defeated by an enemy, and if they return to you, praise your name, and entreat you in this temple, listen in heaven and forgive the sin of your people Israel, and bring them back to the land you gave their fathers.

"If the sky is closed, so that there is no rain, because they have sinned against you and you afflict them, and if then they repent of their sin, and pray, and praise your name in this place, listen in heaven, and forgive the word of your servant and of your people Israel, teaching them the right way to live and sending rain upon this land of yours which you have given to your people as their heritage.

"If there is famine in the land or pestilence; or if blight comes or mildew, or a locust swarm, or devouring insects; if an enemy of your people besieges them in one of their cities; whatever plague or sickness there may be, if then any one [of your entire people Israel] has remorse of conscience and offers some prayer or petition, stretching out his hands toward this temple, listen from your heavenly dwelling place and forgive. You who alone knows the hearts of all men, render to each one of them according to his conduct; knowing their hearts, so treat them that they may fear you as long as they live on the land you gave our fathers.

"To the foreigner likewise, who is not of your people Israel, but comes from a distant land to honor you (since men will learn of your great name and your mighty hand and your outstretched arm), when he comes and prays toward this temple, listen from your heavenly dwelling. Do all that the foreigner asks of you, that all the people of the earth may know your name, may fear you as do your people Israel, and may acknowledge that this temple which I have built is dedicated to your honor.

" Whatever the direction in which you may send your people forth to war against their enemies, if they pray to you, O LORD, toward the city you have chosen and the temple I have built in your honor, listen in heaven to their prayer and petition, and defend their cause.

"When they sin against you (for there is no man who does not sin), and in your anger against them you deliver them to the enemy, so that their captors deport them to a hostile land, far or near, may they repent in the land of their captivity and be converted. If then they entreat you in the land of their captors and say, 'We have sinned and done wrong; we have been wicked'; if with their whole heart and soul they turn back to you in the land of their enemies who took them captive, pray to you toward the land you gave their fathers, the city you have chosen, and the temple I have built in your honor, listen from your heavenly dwelling. Forgive your people their sins and all the offenses they have committed against you, and grant them mercy before their captors, so that these will be merciful towards them. For they are your people and your inheritance, whom you brought out of Egypt, from the midst of an iron furnace.

"Thus may your eyes be open to the petition of your servant and to the petition of your people Israel. Hear them whenever they call upon you, because you have set them apart among all the peoples of the earth for your inheritance, as you declared through your servant Moses when you brought your fathers out of Egypt, O LORD God."

When Solomon finished offering this entire prayer of petition to the LORD, he rose from before the altar of the LORD, where he had been kneeling with is hands outstretched toward heaven.

1 Kings 8:22-54

King Solomon after building the temple offers his prayer to God. He asks for pardon for the Israelite people. He asks for proper judgement of the good and evil. Solomon asks that God listen to people-their petition and prayer especially when they have sinned. God's temple on earth, apart from his heavenly dwelling place was meant as a symbol of the contract God made with the Israelites to help and support them. When they obeyed God and repented of their sin, Solomon's prayer is heard by God.

# Judith's Prayers

Judith threw herself down prostrate, with ashes strewn upon her head, and wearing nothing over her sackcloth. While the incense was being offered in the temple of God in Jerusalem that evening, Judith prayer to the LORD with a loud voice: "LORD, God of my forefather Simeon! You put a sword into his hand to take revenge upon the foreigners who had immodestly loosened the maiden's girdle, shamefully exposed her thighs, and disgracefully violated her body. This they did, though you forbade it. Therefore you had their rulers slaughtered; and you covered with their blood the bed in which they lay deceived, the same bed that had felt the shame of their own deceiving. You smote the slaves together with their princes, and the princes together with their servants. Their wives you handed over to plunder, and their daughters to captivity; and all the spoils you divided among your favored sons, who burned with zeal for you, and in their abhorrence of the defilement of their kinswoman, called on you for help.

O God, my God, hear me also a widow. It is you who were author of those vents and of what preceded and followed them. The present, also, and the future you have planned. Whatever you devise comes into being; the things you decide on come forward and say, 'Here we are!' All your ways are in readiness, and your judgment is made with foreknowledge.

Here are the Assyrians, a vast force, priding themselves on horse and rider, boasting of the power of their infantry, trusting in shield and spear, bow and sling. They do not know that "'You the LORD, crush warfare; Lord is your name.' Shatter their strength in your might, and crush their force in your wrath; for they have resolved to profane your sanctuary, to defile the tent where your glorious name resides, and to overthrow with iron the horns of your altar. See their pride, and send forth your wrath upon their heads. Give me, a widow, the strong hand to execute my plan. With the guile of my lips, smite the slave together with the ruler, the ruler together with his servant; crush their pride by the hand of a woman.

"Your strength is not in numbers, nor does your power depend upon stalwart men; but you are the God of the lowly, the helper of the oppressed, the supporter of the weak, the protector of the forsaken, the savior of those without hope.

"Please, please, God of my forefather, God of the heritage of Israel, LORD of heaven and earth, Creator of the waters, King of all you have created, hear my prayer! Let my guileful speech bring wound and wale on those who have planned dire things against your covenant, your holy temple, Mount Zion, and the homes your children have inherited. Let you whole nation and all the tribes know clearly that you are the God of all power and might, and that there is no other who protects the people of Israel but you alone."

Judith 9:1-14 Judith's Prayers

Then the servants of Holofernes led her into the tent, where she slept to midnight. In the night watch just before dawn, she rose and sent his message to Holofernes, "Give orders, my lord, to let your handmaid go out for prayer." So Holofernes ordered his bodyguard not to hinder her. Thus she stayed in the camp three days. Each night she went out to the ravine of Bethulia, where she washed herself at the spring of the camp. After bathing, she besought the LORD, the God of Israel, to direct her way for the triumph of his people. Then she returned purified to the tent, and remained there until her food was brought to her towards evening.

Judith 12:5-9

She had ordered her maid to stand outside the bedroom and wait, as on the other days, for her to come out; she said she would be going out for her prayer. To Bagoas she had said this also. When all had departed, and no one small or great, was left in the bedroom she said within herself: "O LORD, God of all might, in this hour look graciously on my understanding for the exultation of Jerusalem; now is the time for aiding your heritage and for carrying out my design to shatter the enemies who have risen against us."

Judith 13:3-5

Judith was a widow, a jew, who saved her people from the onslaught of the Assyrian army by decapitating its leader Holofrenes. The book of Judith includes the prayer of the Jewish people for deliverance from the Assyrian Army (Judith 9:1-15). It also includes the prayer of Judith (Judith 9:1-14) where she prays to God to save her people. Her prayer is answered and the people saved.

# The Prayer of Jesus

When Jesus had said this, he raised his eyes to heaven and said, " Father the hour has come. Give glory to your son, so that your son may glorify you, just as you gave him authority over all people, so that he may give eternal life to all you gave him. Now this is eternal life, that they should know you, the only true God, and the one whom you sent, Jesus Christ. I glorified you on earth by accomplishing the work that you gave me to do. Now glorify me, Father, with you, with the glory that I had with you before the world began.

"I revealed your name to those whom you gave me out of the world. The belonged to you, and you gave them to me, and they have kept your word. Now they know that everything you gave me is from you, because the words you gave me I have given to them, and they accepted them and truly understood that I came from you, and they believed that you sent me. I pray for them. I do not pray for the world but for the ones that you have given me, because they are yours, and every thing of mind is yours and everything of yours is mine, and I have been glorified in them. And now I will no longer be in the world, but they are in the world, while I am coming to you. Holy Father, keep them in your name that you have given me, so that they may be one just as we are. When I was with them I protected them in your name that you gave me, and I guarded them, that none of them was lost except then son of destruction, in order that the scripture might be fulfilled. But now I am coming to you I speak this in the world so that they may share my joy completely. I gave them your word, and the world hated them, because they do not belong to the world any more than I belong to the world. Consecrate them in the truth. Your word is truth. As you sent me into the world, so I sent them into the world. And I consecrate myself for them, so that they may also be consecrated in truth.

"I pray not only for them, but also for those who will believe in me through their word, so that they may all be one, as you, Father, are in me and I in you, that they also may be in us, that the world may also believe that you sent me. And I have given them the glory you gave me, so that they may be one, as we are one, I in them, and you in me, that they may be brought to perfection as one, that the world may know that you sent me, and that you loved them even as you loved me. Father, they are your gift to me. I wish that where I am they also may be me, because you loved me before the foundation of the world. Righteous Father, the world does not know you, but I know you, and they know that you sent me. I made known to them your name and I will make it known, that the love with which you loved me may be in them and I in them."

John 17:1-26

In this prayer Jesus the son of God prays to God the Father-God praying to God. Jesus prays to God the Father that his followers might be kept from evil and consecrated to the truth.

# The Prayers of Mordecai and Esther

Mordechai refuses to bow to Haman and becomes the target of Haman's animosity who vows to destroy all of the Jews as well as Mordechai. Queen Esther, foster daughter to Mordechai, and Mordechai pray to God to save the themselves and all the Jews.

Mordechai went away and did exactly as Esther had commanded. Recalling all that the LORD had done, he prayed to him and said: "O Lord God, almighty King, all things are in your power, and there is no one to oppose you in your will to save Israel.

You made heaven and earth and every wonderful thing under the heavens. You are LORD of all, and there is no one who can resist you, LORD. You know all things. You know, O LORD, that it was not out of insolence or pride or desire for fame that I acted thus not bowing down to the proud Haman. Gladly would I have kissed the soles of his feet for the salvation of Israel. But I acted as I did so as not to place the honor of man above that of God. I will not bow down to anyone but you, my LORD> It is not out of pride that I am acting thus. And now, LORD God, King, God of Abraham, spare your people, for our enemies plan our ruin and are bent upon destroying the inheritance that was yours from the beginning. DO not spurn your portion, which you redeemed for yourself out of Egypt. Hear my prayer; have pity on your inheritance and turn our sorrow into joy: thus shall we live to sing praise to your name. O LORD. Do not silence those who praise you."

Queen Esther, seized with mortal anguish, likewise had recourse to the LORD> Taking off her splendid garments, she put on garments of distress and mourning. IN place of her ointments she covered her head with dirt and ashes. She afflicted her body severely; all her festive adornments were put aside, and her hair was wholly disheveled.

Then she prayed to the LORD, the God of Israel, saying: "My LORD, our king, you alone are God. Help me, who am alone and have no help but you, for I am taking my life in my hand. As a child I was wont to hear from the people of the land of my fore-fathers that you, O LORD, chose Israel from among all peoples, and our fathers from among all their ancestors, as a lasting heritage, and that you fulfilled all your promises to them. But now we have sinned in your sight, and you have delivered us into the hands of our enemies, because we worshipped their gods. You are just O LORD. But now they are not satisfied with our bitter servitude, but have undertaken to do away with the decree that you have pronounced, and to destroy your heritage; to close the mouths of those who praise you, and to extinguish the glory of your temple and your altar; to open the mouths of the heathen to acclaim their false gods and to extol and earthly king forever.

O LORD, do not relinquish your scepter to those that are nought. Let them not gloat over our ruin, but turn their own counsel against them and make an example of our chief enemy. Be mindful of us, O LORD. Manifest yourself in the time of our distress and give me courage, King of gods and Ruler of every power. Put in my mouth persuasive words in the presence of the lion and turn his heart to hatred for our enemy, so that he and those who are in league with him may perish. Save us by your power, and help me, who am alone and have no one but you O LORD.

You Know all things. You know that I hate the glory of the pagans, and abhor the bed of the uncircumcised or of any foreigner. You know that I am under constraint, that I abhor the sign of grandeur which rests on my head when I appear in public; abhor it like a polluted rag, and do not wear

it in private. I, your handmaid, have never eaten at
the table of Haman, nor have I graced the banquet of
the king or drunk the wine of libations. From the day
I was brought here till now, your handmaid has had
no joy except in you, O LORD, God of Abraham. O
God, more powerful than all, hear the voice of those
in despair. Save us from the power of the wicked, and
deliver me from my fear.

ON the third day, putting and end to her
prayers, she took off her penitential garments and
arrayed herself in her royal attire.

Esther C1-D1

Queen Esther is called upon to change Haman's
counsel to the king to kill all the Jews and thereby save
them. Mordecai, her relative also prays for salvation
of the Jews. The result is the death of Haman and a
Jewish uprising which saves the Jews. The prayer of
Mordecai and Esther is heard.

Jehosaphat stood up in the assembly of Judah
and Jerusalem in the house of the LORD before
the new court, and he said: "LORD, God of our
ancestors, are you not God in heaven, and do you
not rule over all the kingdoms of the nations? In your
hand is power and might, and no one can withstand
you. Was it not you, our God, who dispossessed the
inhabitants of the land before your people Israel and
gave it forever to the descendants of Abraham your
friend? They have dwelt in it and built in it a sanctuary
for your name. They have said: If veil comes upon us,
the sword of judgement, or pestilence, or famine, we

will stand before this house and before you, for your name is in this house, and we will cry out to you in our affliction, and you will hear and save! And now, see the Ammonites, Moabites, and those of Mount Seir whom you did not allow Israel to invade when they came from the land of Egypt, but instead they passed them by and did not destroy them: See how they are now repaying us by coming to drive us out of the possession you have given us. O our God, will you not bring judgement on them? We are powerless, before this vast multitude that is coming against us. We ourselves do not know what to do, so our eyes are turned towards you."

Jehosaphat prays for relief against the peoples who were attacking Israel.

2 Chronicles 20:5-12

## Solomon's Prayer

Solomon then took his place before the altar of the Lord in the presence of the whole community of Israel and stretched forth his hands. He had made a bronze platform five cubits long, five cubits wide, and five cubits high, which he had placed in the center of the courtyard. Having ascended it, Solomon knelt in the presence of the whole of Israel and stretched forth his hands toward heaven… Thus he prayed:

"LORD, God of Israeli, there is no God like you in heaven or on earth: you keep your covenant and show kindness to your servants who are wholeheartedly faithful to you. You have kept the promise you made to my father David, your servant. With your own mouth you spoke it, and by your own hand you have brought it to fulfillment this day. Now, therefore, LORD, God of Israel, keep the further promise you made to my father David, your servant, when you said, 'You shall always have someone from your line to sit before me on the throne of Israel, provided only that your descendants look to their conduct so as to always live according to my law, even as you have lived in my presence.' Now, LORD, God of Israel, may this promise which you made to your servant David be confirmed.

"Can it indeed be that God dwells with mankind on earth? If the heavens and the highest heavens cannot contain you, how much less this temple which I have built! Look kindly on the prayer and petition of your of your servant, O LORD, my God, and listen to the cry of supplication your servant makes before you. May your eyes watch day and night over this temple, the place where you have decreed you shall be honored; may you heed the prayer which I your servant offer toward this place. Listen to the petitions of your servant and of your people Israel, which they direct toward this place. Listen from your heavenly dwelling, and when you have heard, pardon.

When any man sins against his neighbor and is required to take on oath of execration against himself, and when he comes for the oath before your altar in this temple, listen from heaven: take action and pass judgement on your servants, requiting the wicked man and holding him responsible for his conduct, but absolving the innocent and rewarding him according to his virtue. When your people Israel have sinned against you and are defeated by the enemy, but afterward they return and praise your name, and they pray to you and entreat you in this temple, listen from heaven and forgive the sin of your people Israel, and bring them back to the land which you gave them and their fathers. When the sky is closed so that there is no rain, because they have sinned against you, but then they pray toward this place and praise your name, and they withdraw from sin because you afflict them, listen in heaven and forgive the sin of your servant and your people Israel. But teach them the right way to live, and send rain upon your land which you gave their people as their heritage. When there is famine in the land, when there is pestilence, or blight, or mildew, or locusts, or caterpillars; when their enemies besiege them at any on their gate; whenever there is a plague or sickness of any kind; when any Israelite of all your people offers a payer or petition of any kind, and in awareness of his affliction and pain, stretches out his hands towards toward this temple, listen from your heavenly dwelling place and forgive. Knowing his heart, render to everyone according tohis conduct, for you alone known the hearts of men. So may they fear you and walk in your ways as long as they live on the land you gave our fathers.

For the foreigner, too, who is not of your people Israel, when he comes from a distant land to honor your great name, your mighty power, and your outstretched arm, when they come in prayer to this temple, listen from your heavenly dwelling place, and do whatever the foreigner entreats you, that all the peoples of the earth may know your name, fearing you as do your people Israel, and knowing that this house which I have built is dedicated to your honor.

When your people go forth to war against their enemies, wherever you send them, and pray to you in the direction of this city and the house I have built in your honor, listen from heaven to their prayer and petition, and defend their cause. When they sin against you (for there is no man who does not sin), and in your anger against them you deliver them to the enemy, so that their captors deport them to another land, far or near, when they repent in the land where they are captive and are converted, when they entreat you in the land of their captivity and say, 'We have sinned and done wrong; we have been wicked,' and with their whole heart and with their while soul they turn back to you in the land of those who hold them captive, when they pray in the direction of their land which you gave their fathers, and of the city which you have chose, and of the house which I built to your honor, listen from your heavenly dwelling place, hear their prayers and petitions, and uphold their cause. Forgive your people who have sinned against you. My God, may your eyes be open and your ears attentive to the prayer of this place. And now, "Advance, LORD God to your resting place, you and the ark of your majesty. May your priests, LORD God, be clothed with salvation, may your faithful ones rejoice in good things. LORD God, reject not the plea of your anointed, remember the devotion of David, your servant."

After Solomon finished building the temple of the LORD, the royal palace, and everything else that he had planned, the LORD appeared to him a second time, as he had appeared to him in Gibeon. The LORD said to him: I have heard the prayer of petition which you offered in my presence. I have consecrated this temple which you have built; I confer my name upon it forever, and my eyes and my heart shall be there always. AS for you, if you live in my presence as your father David lived, sincerely and uprightly, doing just as I have commanded you, keeping my statutes and decrees, I will establish your throne of sovereignty over Israel forever, as I promised your father David when I said, 'You shall always have someone from your line on the throne of Israel.' But if you and your descendants ever withdraw from me, fail to keep the commandments and statutes which I set before you, and proceed to venerate and worship strange gods, I will cut Israel from the land I gave them and repudiate the temple I have consecrated to my honor. Israel shall become a proverb and byword among all nations, and this temple shall become a heap of ruins. Every passerby shall catch his breath in amazement, and ask, 'Why has the LORD done this to the land and to this temple?' Men will answer: They forsook the LORD, their God, who brough their fathers out of the land of Egypt; they adopted strange gods which they worshiped and served. That is why the LORD has brought down upon them all this evil.'"

1 Kings 9: 1-3

When Solomon had ended his prayer, fire came down from heaven and consumed the holocaust and the sacrifices, and the glory of the LORD filled the house.

2 Chronicles 6:12-7:1

The Lord appeared to Solomon during the night and said to him: "I have heard your prayer, and I have chosen this place for my house of sacrifice. If I close heaven so that there is no rain, if I command the locust to devour the land, if I send pestilence among my people, and if my people, upon whom my name has been pronounced, humble themselves and pray, and seek my presence and turn from their evil ways, I will hear them from heaven and pardon their sins and revive their land. Now my eyes shall be open and my ears attentive to the prayer of this place. And now I have chosen and consecrated this house that my name may be there forever; my eyes and my heart also shall be there always."

2 Chronicles 7: 12-16

# Prayer melts away anxiety

"Rejoice in the Lord always. I shall say it again: rejoice! Your kindness should be known to all. The Lord is near. Have no anxiety at all, but in everything, by prayer and petition, with thanksgiving, make your requests known to God. Then the peace of God that surpasses all understanding will guard your hearts and minds in Christ Jesus."

Philippians 4:4-7

When we pray about things we are anxious about it focuses the mind on those things and the mind comes up with solutions. The solutions usually make us less anxious. Moreover when we give the things we are anxious about up to God and let him help solve our problems we end up with divine solutions. In the end all we need are our food and clothing and God promises that he will give us these.

Everyone gets anxious and our anxieties can overwhelm us or even kill us. God promises that if we pray our anxieties will be replaced with his true peace in Jesus. We should make a list of our needs in the form of a petition and give this too up to God. Thanksgiving for what God does give us is only right.

# To Have Others Pray for Us

"Pray for us, for we are confident that we have a clear conscience, wishing to act rightly in every respect. I especially ask for your prayers that I may be restored to you very soon."

Hebrews 13:18-19

Whether we are sick or looking for a new job or making an important decision, we can always ask for someone to pray to God for us. This act of goodwill-others praying for our best interests is always helpful. It lessens our anxieties and adds to our pleadings before God. The above verse is specific in that it states we should pray with a clear conscience. Our prayers becomes holy before God when we pray with a clear conscience. When prayer request involves more than one person, it is good to have others in that prayer request pray for the same thing.

# Prayer-In Agony
# Before Death

Then going out he went, as was his custom, to the Mount of Olives, and the disciples followed him. When he arrived at the place he said to them, "pray that you may not undergo the test." After withdrawing about a stone's throw from them and knelling, he prayed, saying, "Father, if you are willing, take this cup from me; still, not my will but yours be done." [And to strengthen him and angel from heaven appeared to him. He was in such agony and he prayed so fervently that his sweat became like drops of blood falling on the ground.] When he rose from prayer and returned to his disciples, he found them sleeping from grief. He said to them, "Why are you sleeping? Get up and pray that you might not undergo the test."

Luke 22:39-46

Then they came to a place named Gethsemane, and he said to his disciples, "Sit here while I pray." He took with hm Peter, James, and John and began to be troubled and distressed. Then he said to them, "My soul is sorrowful even to death. Remain here and keep watch." He advances a little and fell to the ground and prayed that if it were possible the hour might pass by him; he said, "Abba, Father, all things are possible to you. Take this cup away from me, but not what I will but what you will." When he returned he found them asleep. He said to Pete, "Simon, are you asleep? Could you not keep watch for one hour? Watch and pray that you may not undergo the test. The spirit is willing but the flesh is weak." Withdrawing again, he prayed, saying the same thing. Then he returned once more and found them asleep, for they could not keep their eyes open and did not know what to answer him. He returned a third time and said to them, " Are you still sleeping and taking your rest? It is enough. The hour has come. Behold, the Son of man is to be handed over to sinners. Get up let us go. See my betrayer is at hand."

Mark 14:32-42

Then Jesus came with them to a place called Gethsemane, and said to his disciples, "Sit here while I go over there and pray." He took along Peter and the two sons of Zebedee, and began to feel sorrow and distress. Then he said to them, "My soul is sorrowful even to death. Remain and keep watch with me." He advanced a little and fell prostrate in prayer, saying, "My father, if it is possible, let this cup pass from me; yet, not as I will, but as you will." When he returned to his disciples he found them asleep. He said to Peter, "So you could not keep watch with me for one hour? Watch and pray that you may not undergo the tests. The spirit is willing but the flesh is weak." "Withdrawing a second time, he prayed again, "My Father, if it is not possible that this cup pass without my drinking it, your will be done!" Then he returned once more and found them asleep, for they could not keep their eyes open. He left them and withdrew again and prayed a third time, saying the same thing again. Then he returned to his disciples and said to them, "Are you still sleeping and taking your rest? Behold, the hour is at hand when the son of man is to be handed over to sinners. Get up, let us go. Look, my betrayer is at hand."

Matthew 26:36-46

The above three passages reference Jesus's agony in the Garden. This is just before Jesus's betrayal and Arrest days before his death on the cross. Jesus knows he will suffer and die. He asks God the Father to stop the process and let him live. After praying Jesus accepts God's will and plan. Jesus probably prayed for his disciples, and for strength and courage. He prayed also that his disciples not undergo the test. This probably references their own deaths.

# Prayer-In the Spirit

In the same way, the spirit too comes to the aid of our weakness; for we do not know how to pray as we ought, but the spirit itself intercedes with inexpressible groanings.

Romans 8:26

# Prayer-Devotion to Prayer

They devoted themselves to the teaching of the apostles and to the communal life, to the breaking of the bread and to the prayers.

Acts 2:42

At that time, as the number of disciples continued to grow, the Hellenists complained against the Hebrews because their widows were being neglected in the daily distribution. So the twelve called together the community of the disciples and said, "It is not right for us to neglect the word of God to serve at table. Brothers, select from among you seven reputable men, filled with the spirit and wisdom, whom we shall appoint to the task, whereas we shall devote ourselves to prayer and to the ministry of the word" The proposal was acceptable to the whole community, so they chose Stephen, a man filled with faith and the holy spirit, also Philip, Prochorus, Nicanor, Timon, Parmenas, and Nicholas of Antioch, a convert to Judaism. They presented these men to the apostles who prayed and laid hands of them. The word of the God continued to spread, and the number of the disciples in Jerusalem increased greatly; even a large group of priests were becoming obedient to the faith.

Acts 6-1-7

# Prayer-Healing Others

Paul visited him and, after praying, laid his hands on him and healed him. After this had taken place, the rest of the sick on the island came to Paul and were cured.

Acts 28:19

# Prayer-Restoring Life

Now in Joppa there was a disciple named Tabitha (Which translated means Dorcas). She was completely occupied with good deeds and almsgiving. Now during those days she fell sick and died, so after washing her, they laid [her] out in a room upstairs. Since Lydda was near Joppa, the disciples, hearing that Peter was there, sent two men to him with the request, " Please come to us without delay." So Peter got up and went with them. When he arrived, they took him to the room upstairs where all the widows came to him weeping and showing him the tunics and cloaks that Dorcas had made while she was with them. Peter sent them all out and knelt down and prayed. Then he turned to her body and said, "Tabitha, rise up." She opened her eyes, saw Peter, and sat up. He gave her his hand and raised her up, and when he had called the holy ones and the widows, he presented her alive. This became known all over Joppa, and many came to believe in the Lord. And he stayed a long time in Joppa with Simon, a tanner.

Acts 9:36-43

## Prayer-Where to Pray

On the Sabbath we went outside the city gate along the river where we thought there would be a place of prayer.

Acts 16:13

## Prayer-Close to God

There was also a prophetess, Anna, the daughter of Phanuel, of the tribe of Asher. She was advanced in years, having lived seven years with her husband after her marriage, and then as a widow until she was eighty four. She never left the temple, but worshipped night and day with fasting and prayer. And coming forward at that very time, she gave thanks to God and spoke about the child to all who were awaiting the redemption of Jerusalem.

Luke 2:36-38

# Prayer-God hears prayer

But we prayed to the LORD, and our prayer was heard; we offered sacrifices and fine flour; we lighted the lamps and set out the loaves of bread.

2 Maccabees 1:8

Now in Caesarea there was a man named Cornelius, a centurion of the Cohort called the Italica, devout an God-fearing along with the whole household, who used to give alms generously to the Jewish people and pray to God constantly. One afternoon about three o'clock, he saw plainly in a vision an angel of God come in to him and say to him, "Cornelius"> He looked intently at him and seized with fear, said, "What is it sir?" He said to him, "Your prayers and almsgiving have ascended as a memorial offering before God. Now send some men to Joppa and summon one Simon who is called Peter. He is staying with another Simon, a tanner, who has a house by the sea."

Acts 10:1-6

Cornelius replied, "Four days ago at this hour, three o'clock in the afternoon, I was at prayer in my house when suddenly a man in dazzling robes stood before me and said, Cornelius, your prayer has been heard and your almsgiving remembered before God. Send therefore to Joppa and summon Simon who is called Peter. He is a guest in the house of Simon, a tanner, by the sea'"

Acts 1030-32

Then, when the whole assembly of the people was praying outside at the hour of the incense offering, the angel of the Lord appeared to him standing at the right of the altar of incense. Zechariah was troubled by what he saw, and fear came upon him. But the angel said to him, "Do not be afraid, Zechariah, because your prayer has been heard. Your wife Zechariah will bear you a son, and you shall name him John.

Luke1:10-13

## Prayer-God is pleased

After all the people had been baptized and Jesus also had been baptized and was praying, heaven was opened and the holy Spirit descended upon him in bodily form like a dove. And a voice came from heaven, "You are my beloved Son; with you I am well pleased."

# Prayer in the psalms

Answer when I call, my saving God. In my troubles, you cleared a way; show me favor; hear my prayer.

Psalm 4:2

Hear my cry for help, my king, my God! To you I pray O LORD.

Psalm 5:3

Hear, LORD, my pleas for justice; pay heed to my cry; Listen to my prayer spoken without guile.

Psalm 17:1

O God, hear my prayer. Listen to the words of my mouth.

Psalm 54:4

LORD of hosts, how long will you burn with anger while your people pray.

Psalm 80:5

Heeding the plea of the lowly, not scorning their prayer.

Psalm 102:18

LORD, hear my prayer, let my cry come to you.

Psalm 102-2

The book of psalms is the most important book in the bible to teach us how to pray. The book is in fact a collection of prayers that serve as a template for our own prayers. Specifically the word prayer is explicitly written in the above sections of the psalms. Most of these ask God to hear our prayers.

## Prayer-Prayer When Sick

My son, when you are ill, do not delay, but pray to God, for it is he who heals.

Sirach 38:9

There are times that give him an advantage, and he too beseeches God that his diagnosis may be correct and his treatment bring about a cure.

Sirach 38:13-14

Therefore, confess your sins to one another and pray for one another, that you might he healed.

James 5:16

It so happened that the father of Publius was sick with a fever and dysentery. Paul visited him, and after praying, laid his hands on him and healed him.

In those days, when Hezekiah was mortally ill, the prophet Isiah, son of Amoz, came and said to him: "Thus says the LORD: "Put your house in order, for you are about to die: you shall not recover.' He turned his face to the wall and prayed to the LORD: "O LORD, remember how faithfully and wholeheartedly I conducted myself in your presence, doing what was pleasing to you!" And Hezekiah wept bitterly.

Before Isaiah had left the central courtyard, the word of the LORD came to him: "Go back and tell Hezekiah, the leader of my people: 'Thus says the LORD, the God of your forefather David: I have heard your prayer and seen your tears. I will heal you. IN three you shall go up to the LORD's temple; I will add fifteen years to your life. I will rescue you and this city from the hand of the king of Assyria; I will be a shield to this city for my own sake, and the sake of my servant David.'"

Isaiah the ordered a poultice of figs to be brought and applied to the boil, that he might recover. Then Hezekiah asked Isaiah, "What is the sign that the LORD will heal me and that I shall go up to the temple of the LORD on the third day?" Isaiah replied, "This will be the sign from the LORD that he will do what he has promised: Shall the shadow go forward or back ten steps?"

"It is easy for the shadow to advance ten steps," Hezekiah answered. "Rather, let it go back ten steps."

So the prophet Isaiah invoked the LORD, who made the shadow retreat the ten steps it had descended on the staircase to the terrace of Ahaz.

2 Kings 20:1-11

In those days, when Hezekiah was mortally ill, the prophet Isaiah, son of Amoz, came and said to him: "Thus says the LORD: Put your affairs in order, for you are about to die; you shall not recover." Hezekiah turned his face to the wall and prayed to the LORD: Ah, LORD remember how faithfully and wholeheartedly I conducted myself in your presence, doing what was good in your sight!" And Hezekiah wept bitterly. Then the word of the LORD came to Isaiah!. Go tell Hezekiah: Thus says the LORD, the God of your father David: I have heard your prayer; I have seen your tears. Now I will add fifteen years to your life. I will rescue you and this city from the hand of the king of Assyria; I will be a shield to this city.

Isaiah 38: 1-6

# Prayer-Why Pray

## Some other prayers

The fervent prayer of a righteous person is very powerful. Elijah was a human being like us; yet he prayed earnestly that it might not rain, and for three years and six months it did not rain upon the land. Then he prayed again, and the sky gave rain and the earth produced its fruit.

James 5:16-18

# Prayer-Lord Hear Our Prayer

Hear the prayer of your servants, according to your good will toward your people. Thus all the ends of the earth will know that you are the eternal God.

Sirach 37:22

LORD, hear my prayer; in your faithfulness listen to my pleading; answer me in your righteousness.

Psalm 143:1

LORD, hear my prayer; let my cry come to you.

Psalm 102:2t

Heeding the plea of the lowly, not scorning their prayer.

Psalm 102:18

Hear, LORD, my plea for justice; pay heed to my cry; Listen to my prayer from lips without guile.

Psalm 17:1

O God, by your name save me. BY your strength defend my cause. O God, hear my prayer. Listen to the words of my mouth.

Psalm 54:3-4

One of the most important prayers we can say is one where we ask for God to hear our prayer. The above prayers in the book of psalms and Sirach give examples where we ask God to hear our prayers.

The above prayers are remarkable in that they represent themselves as servants of God, lowly, and people with a cause.

# Pray for Enemies

**"You have heard it said, 'You shall love your neighbor and hate your enemy.' But I say to you, love your enemies, and pray for those who persecute you, that you may be children or your heavenly Father, for he makes his sun rise on the bad and the good, and causes rain to fall on the just and the unjust."**

**Matthew 5:43-45**

**" But to you who hear I say, love your enemies, do good to those who hate you, bless those who curse you, pray for those who mistreat you."**

**Luke 6:27-28**

Jesus makes it quite clear that he wants us to pray for our enemies, those who persecute and mistreat us. Who knows-if we pray for our enemies maybe they might even become our friends.

God loves everyone and wants us to come to him. God's love for those who hate him is shown by us when we love our enemies and pray for them. When we pray for someone who mistreats us it changes the dynamic from one of mutual hostility to one where the other's mistreatment no longer effects us. When we pray for our enemies our hatred for them dissolves. This praying for enemies is also very beneficial physiologically and mentally. Our good will to other people, when we pray for them, takes away the need for an 'ax to grind'. All the negative energy that goes into retribution and retaliation is lost forever.

## Prayer that God hears

**He then addressed this parable to those who were convinced of their own righteousness and despised everyone else. "Two people went up to the temple area to pray: one was a Pharisee and the other was a tax collector. The Pharisee took up his position and spoke this prayer to himself. 'O God, I thank you that I am not like the rest of humanity-greedy, dishonest, adulterous-or even like this tax**

collector. I fast twice a week, and I pay tithes on my whole income. But the tax collector stood off at a distance and would not even raise his eyes to heaven but beat his breast and prayed, 'O God be merciful to me a sinner.' I tell you, the latter went home justified, not the former; for everyone who exalts himself will be humbled, and the one who humbles himself will be exalted."

God does not want us to tell him in our prayer how great or important we are. If we pray our faults and failures he might even have the grace and opportunity to forgive u. Prayer meant to show how much better we are than other people probably is not heard.

# Miscellaneous Prayers
# New Testament

Be vigilant at all times and pray that you have the strength to escape the tribulations that are imminent and to stand before the Son of Man.

Luke 22:36

"Simon, Simon, behold Satan has demanded to sift all of you like wheat, but I have prayed that your own faith may not fail; and once you have turned back, you must strengthen your brothers."

Luke 22:31

Then children were brought to him that he might lay his hands on them and pray.

Matthew 19:13

With trust in your compliance I write to you, knowing that you will do even more than I say. At the same time prepare a guest room for me, for I hope to be granted to you through prayers.

Philemon 21-22

Rejoice in the Lord always. I shall say it again : rejoice! Your kindness should be known to all. The Lord is near. Have no anxiety at all, but in everything, by prayer and petition, with thanksgiving, make your requests known to God. Then the peace of God that surpasses all understanding will guard your hearts and minds in Christ Jesus.

Philippians 4:4-7

After all the people had been baptized and Jesus also had been baptized and was praying, heaven was opened and the holy Spirit descended upon him in bodily form like a dove. And a voice came from heaven, "You are my beloved Son; with you I am well pleased."

Luke 3:21-22

The heart can reveal your situation better than seven sentinels on a tower. Then with all this, pray to God to make your steps firm in the true path.

Sirach 37:14-15

As a result, all the people dreaded the LORD and Samuel. They said to Samuel, "Pray to the LORD your God for us, your servants, that we may not die for having added to all our other sins the evil of asking for a king." "Do not fear", Samuel answered them. " It is true that you have committed all this evil; still, you must not turn from the LORD, but must worship him with your whole heart. Do not turn to meaningless idols which can neither profit nor save; they are nothing. For the sake of his great name the LORD will not abandon his people, since the LORD himself chose to make you his people. As for me, far be it from me to sin against the LORD by ceasing to pray for you and to teach you the good and right way. But you must fear the LORD and worship his faithfully with your whole heart; keep in mind the great things he has done among you. If instead you continue to do evil, both you and your king shall perish."

Samuel 12:18-25

While Ezra prayed and acknowledged their guilt, weeping and prostrate before the house of God,, a very large assembly of Israelites gathered about him, men, women, and children; and the people wept profusely.

Ezra 10:1

"Please grant our petition; pray for us to the LORD, your God for all this remnant. As you see, only a few of us remain, but once were many. May the LORD, your God, show us the way we should take, and what we should do. "Very well!" Jerimiah the prophet answered them: "I will pray to the LORD your God, as you desire; whatever the LORD answers I will tell you; I will withhold nothing from you."

Jerimiah 42:2-4

All of Jonathan's men fled; no one stayed except the army commanders Mattathias, son of Absalom, and Judas, son of Chalphi. Jonathan, tore his robes, threw dust on his head, and prayed.

1 Maccabees 11: 70-71

Prayer from the lips of the poor is heard at once, and justice quickly granted them.

Sirach 21:5

"You have chosen this house to bear your name, to be a house of prayer and petition for your people. Take revenge on this man and his army, and let them fall by the sword. Remember their blasphemies, and do not let them continue."

1 Maccabees 7:37-38

"Save me, I pray, from the hand of my brother Esau! Otherwise I fear that when he comes he will strike me down and slay the mothers and children."

Genesis 32:12

This bible passage references the first time the word prayer is used in the scriptures. Jacob's brother Esau was homicidally angry with Jacob because he had taken his birthright and his blessing. Jacob left his brother for decades and stared his own family with four wives and many children. Later Jacob decided to leave the place he raised his family and move back near his brother. Fearful that his brother still harbored anger, Jacob said the above prayer.

"Then Pharaoh summoned Moses and Aaron and said, "Pray the LORD to remove the frogs from me and my subjects, and I will let the people go to offer sacrifice to the LORD." Moses answered Pharoah, "Do me the favor of appointing the time when I am to pray for you and your servants and your subjects, that the frogs may be taken away from you and your houses and be left only in the river."

Exodus 8:4-5

The second of the plagues of Egypt was the frogs. At Moses word, God sent frogs to invade Egypt… Pharaoh did not believe in Jewish God but still asked Moses to pray to his God th remove the Gods which he did.

"Manoah then prayed to the LORD, " O LORD, I beseech you," he said, "May the man of God whom you sent, return to us to teach us what to do for the boy who will be born." God heard the prayer of Manoah, and the angel of God came to the woman as she was sitting in the field."

Judges 13:8-9

The above passage tells of the conception and birth of Samson in the book of Judges. Samson's mother was barren and had to children but an angel of the Lord told her that she would bear a son. The woman told her husband of the encounter and her husband prayed that the angel would return which he did. The angel told the parents that they would have a boy who they named Samson.

The story is similar to the story of Samuel and John the Baptist who were born to barren women with no children. These stories are told in the first book of Samuel and the new testament in the book of Luke. Women who are barren and pray to God might be blessed with children.

"In her bitterness she prayed to the LORD, weeping copiously, and she made a vow, promising: "O Lord of hosts, if you look with pity on the misery of your handmaid, if you remember me and do not forget me, if you give your husband a male child, I will give him to the Lord for a long as he lives; neither wine nor liquor shall he drink, and no razor shall ever touch his head." As she remained long at prayer before the LORD. Eli watched her mouth, for Hannah was praying silently; though her lips were moving, her voice could not be heard. Eli, thinking her drunk, said to her, "How long will you make a drunken show of yourself? Sober up from your wine!" It isn't that, my lord," Hannah answered. "I am an unhappy woman. I have had neither wine nor liquor; I was only pouring out my troubles to the LORD. Do not think your handmaid a ne'er-do-well; my prayer has been prompted by my deep sorrow and misery."

1 Samuel 10-16

Hannah was barren and had no children but she prayed to God and was given a son Samuel a central figure in the bible. Eli the priest told her to go in peace and that she be granted what she asked for.

"Thus you will see and understand how greatly the LORD is displeased that you have asked for a king." Samuel then called on the LORD, and the LORD sent thunder and rain that day. As a result, all the people dreaded the LORD and Samuel. They said to Samuel, "Pray to the LORD your God for us, your servants, that we may not die for having added to all our other sins the evil for asking for a king."

1 Samuel 17-19

The Israelites had been led by Moses, then Joshua, then the Judges and then Samuel but the people then wanted a king. Samuel informed the people that in asking for a king, the Israelites might not be all blessed. God tell Samuel to chose a king, and gives the Israelites, Saul. After the Israelites are given Saul, both Samuel and God are angry with the Israelites. The Israelites perceiving that God is angry with them ask Samuel to pray for them to God that God's anger dissipate.

Therefore the LORD brought against them the army commanders of the Assyrian king; they took Manasseh with hooks, shackled him with chains, and transported him to Babylon. In this distress, he began to appease the LORD, his God. He humbled himself abjectly before the God of his fathers and prayed to him. The LORD let himself be won over: he heard his prayer and restored him to his kingdom in Jerusalem. Then Manasseh understood that the LORD is indeed God.

2 Chronicles 33:11-13

Then I proclaimed a fast, there by the river of Ahava, that we might humble ourselves before our God to petition him for a safe journey for ourselves, our children, and all our possessions. For I would have been ashamed to ask the king for troops and horsemen to protect us against enemies along the way, since we had said to the king, "The favoring hand of our God is upon all who seek him, but his mighty wrath is against all who forsake him." So we fasted, and prayed to our God for this, and our petition was granted.

Ezra 8:21-23

He rescued us from such great danger of death, and he will continue to rescue us; in him we have put our hope [that] he will also rescue us again, as you help us with prayer, so that thanks may be given by many on our behalf for the gift granted us through the prayers of many.

2 Corinthians 1:10-11

Jesus rescues from death especially when we pray and when others pray for us.

I give thanks to my God at every remembrance of you, praying always with joy in my every prayer for all of you, because of your partnership for the Gospel from the first day until now.

Philippians 1:3-5

The apostle Paul for those who spread the good news of Jesus Christ.

Therefore, from the day we heard this, we do not cease praying for you and asking that you be filled with the knowledge of his will through all spiritual wisdom and understanding to live in a manner worth of the Lord, so as to be fully pleasing, in every good work bearing fruit and growing in the knowledge of God, strengthened with every power, in accord with his glorious might, for all endurance and patience, with joy, giving thanks to the Father who has made you fit to share in the inheritance of the holy ones in light.

Colossians 1:9-12

It is good to pray for the good and well being of other people.

Finally, brothers, pray for us, so that the word of the Lord may speed forward and be glorified, as it did among you, and that we may be delivered from perverse and wicked people, for not all have faith.

2 Thessalonians 3:1-2

Paul prays for the spread of the good news and for deliverance from perverse and wicked people.

First of all, then I ask that supplications, prayers, petitions, and thanksgivings be offered for everyone, for kings and all in authority, that we may lead a quiet and tranquil life in all devotion and dignity.

1 Timothy 2:1-2

Paul prays for tranquility and dignity for everyone.

For everything created by God is good, and nothing is to be rejected when received with thanksgiving, for it is made holy by the invocation of God is prayer.

1 Timothy 4:4-5

Paul states that everything made by God is good and made holy by the invocation of God.

I give thanks to my God always, remembering you in my prayers, as I hear of the love and faith have in the Lord Jesus and for all the Holy Ones, so that your partnership in the faith may become effective in recognizing every good there is in us that leads to Christ.

Philemon 4-6

Paul prays that people may see the good in the Apostles that would lead people to Christ.

The end of all things is at hand. Therefore, be serious and sober for prayers.

1 Peter 4:7

Peter states that our prayers should be serious and made with sobriety.

Early in the morning, as they were walking along, they saw the fig tree withered to its roots. Peter remembered and said to him, "Rabbi, look! The fig tree that you cursed has withered." Jesus said to them in reply, "Have faith in God, Amen, I say to you, whoever says to this mountain, 'Be lifted up and thrown into the sea', and does not doubt in his heart but believes that what he says will happen, it shall be done for him. Therefore I tell you, all that you ask for in prayer, believe that you will receive it and it shall be yours. When you stand to pray, forgive anyone against whom you have a grievance, so that your heavenly Father may in turn forgive you your transgressions."

Mark 12 20-25

Here Jesus emphasizes that we must have belief and faith that our prayers will come true for them to come true. We must also forgive people their trespasses if we want our prayers to come true.

When they came to the disciples, they saw a large crowd around them and scribes arguing with them. Immediately on seeing him, the crowd was utterly amazed. They ran up to him and greeted him. He asked them, "What are you arguing about with them?" Someone from the crowd answered him, "Teacher, I Have brought to you my son possessed by a mute spirit. Whenever it seizes him, it throws him down; he foams at the mouth, grinds his teeth, and becomes rigid. I asked your disciples to drive it out, but they were unable to do so." He said to them in reply, "O faithless generation, how long will I be with you? How long will I endure you? Bring him here to me." They brought the boy to him. And when he saw him, the spirit immediately threw the boy into convulsions. As he fell to the ground, be began to roll around and foam at the mouth. Then he questioned his father, "How long has this been happening to him?" He replied, Since childhood. It has often thrown him into fire and into water to kill him. But if you can do anything, have compassion on us and help us." Jesus said to him, "'If you can!' Everything is possible to one who has faith." Then the boy's father cried out, "I do believe, help my unbelief!" Jesus on seeing a crowd rapidly gathering, rebuked the unclean spirit and said to it, "Mute and deaf spirit, I command you: come out of him and never enter him again!" Shouting and throwing the boy into convulsions, it came out. He became like a corpse, which caused many to say he is dead!" But Jesus took him by the hand, raised him, and he stood out. When he entered the house, his disciples asked him in private, "Why could we not drive it out?" He said to them, "This kind can only come out through prayer."

Mark 9:14-29

There are certain things that can only happen if we pray for them. This is reason enough to constantly prayer and pray for everything we ask for.

He who honors his father is gladdened by children, and when he prays he is heard.

Sirach3:5

Forgive your neighbors injustice; and when you pray, your own sins will be forgiven.

Sirach 28:2

The prayer of the lowly pierces the clouds; it does not rest till it reaches its goal.

Sirach 35:17

But they called upon the Most High God and lifted up their hands to him; He heard the prayer they uttered, and saved them through Isaiah.

Sirach 48:20

I will ever praise your name and be constant in my prayers to you. Thereupon the LORD heard my voice, he listened to my appeal.

Sirach 51:11

Then, when the whole assembly of the people was praying outside at the hour of the incense offering, the angel of the Lord appeared to him, standing at the right of the altar of incense. Zechariah was troubled by what he saw, and fear came upon him. But the angel said to him, "Do not be afraid Zechariah, because your prayer has been heard. Your wife Elizabeth will bear you a son, and you shall name him John.

Luke 1:10-13

And he said to them, "Suppose one of you has a friend to whom he goes at midnight and says, 'Friend, lend me three loaves of bread, for a friend of mine has arrived at my house from a journey and I have nothing to offer him,' and he said in reply from within, 'Do not bother me; the door has already been locked and my children and I are already in bed. I cannot get up to give you anything.' I tell you, if he does not get up to give him the loaves because of their friendship, he will get up to give him whatever he needs because of his persistence.

Luke 11:5-8

"And I tell you, ask and you will receive; seek and you will find; knock and the door will be opened to you. For everyone who asks, receives; and the one who seeks finds; and to the one who knocks, the door will be opened. What father among you would hand his son a snake when he asks for a fish? Or hand him a scorpion when he asks for an egg? If you then, who are wicked, know how to give good gifts to your children, how much more will the Father in heaven give the holy Spirit to those who ask him?"

Luke 11:9-13

"Simon, Simon, behold Satan has demanded to sift all of you like wheat, but I have prayed that your own faith may not fail; and once you have turned back, you must strengthen your brothers."

Luke 22:31-32

Then going out he went, as was his custom, to the Mount of Olives, and the disciples followed him. When he arrived at the place he said to them, "Pray that you might not undergo the test." After withdrawing about a stone's throw from them and kneeling, he prayed, saying, "Father, if you are willing, take this cup away from me; still, not my will but yours be done." [And to strengthen him an angel from heaven appeared to him. He was in such agony and prayed so fervently that his sweat became like drops of blood falling on the ground.] When he rose from prayer and returned to his disciples, he found them sleeping from grief. He said to them, "Why are you sleeping? Get up and pray that you may not undergo the test."

Luke 22:39-46

Their message was: "We send you funds, with which you are to procure holocausts, sin offerings, and frankincense, and to prepare cereal offerings;

offer these on the altar of the LORD our God, and pray for the life of Nebuchadnezzar, king of Babylon, and that of Belshazzar, his son, that their lifetimes may equal the duration of the heavens above the earth; and that the LORD may give us strength, and light to our eyes, that we may live under the protective shadow of Nebuchadnezzar, king of Babylon, and that of Belshazzar, his son, and serve them long, finding favor in their sight. Pray for us also to the LORD, our God; for we have sinned against the LORD, our God, and the wrath and anger of the LORD have not been withdrawn from us at the present day.

Baruch 1:10-13

After giving the deed of purchase to Baruch, son of Neriah, I prayed thus to the LORD: Ah, Lord God, you have made heaven and earth by your great might, with your outstretched arm; nothing is impossible to you. You continue your kindness through a thousand generations; and you repay the father's guilt even to the lap of their sons who follow them. O God, great and mighty, whose name is the LORD of hosts, great in counsel, mighty in deed, whose eyes are open to all the ways of men, giving to each according to his ways, according to the fruit of his deeds: you have wrought signs and wonders in the land of Egypt and to this day, both in Israel and among all other men, until now you have gained renown. With strong hand and outstretched arm you brought your people Israel out of the land of Egypt amid signs and wonders and great terror. This land you gave them, as you promised their fathers under oath, a land flowing with milk and honey. They entered and took possession of it, but they did not listen to your voice; by your law they did not live, and what you commanded they failed to do. Hence you let all these evils befall them. See, the siegeworks have arrived at this city to breach it; the city will be handed over to the Chaldeans who are attacking it, amid sword, famine, and pestilence. What you threatened has happened, you see it yourself; and yet you tell me, O LORD GOD: Buy the field with money, call in witnesses. But the city has already been handed over to the Chaldeans.

Jerimiah 32:16-25

Then Isaiah, son of Amoz sent this message to Hezekiah: Thus says the LORD, the God of Israel: In answer to your prayer for help against Sennacherib, king of Assyria, this is the word the LORD has spoken concerning him: She despises you, laughs you to scorn, the virgin daughter Zion: Behind you she wags her head, daughter Jerusalem. Whom you have insulted and blasphemed, against whom you have raised your voice And lifted up your eyes on high? Against the Holy One of Israel! Through your servants you have insulted the LORD: You said, "With my many chariots I climbed the mountain heights, the recesses of Lebanon; I cut down its lofty cedars, its choice cypresses; I recached the remotest heights, its forest park. I dug wells and drank water in foreign lands; I dried up with the soles of my feet all the rivers of Egypt. Have you not heard? Long ago I prepared it, from days of old I planned it, now I have brought it to pass: That you should reduce fortified cities into heaps of ruins, While their inhabitants, shorn of power, are dismayed and ashamed, Becoming like the plants of the field, like the green growth, like the scorched grass on the housetops, I am aware of whether you stand or sit; I know whether you come or go, and also your rage against me and your fury which has reached my ears, I will put my hook in your nose and my bit in your mouth, and make you return the way you came. This shall be a sign for you: this year you shall eat of the after growth, next year, what grows of itself; But in the third year, sow and reap, plant vineyards and eat their fruit! The remaining survivors of the house of Judah shall again strike root below and bear fruit above. For out of Jerusalem shall come a remnant, and from mount Zion, survivors, The Zeal of the LORD of hosts shall do this. Therefore, thus says the LORD concerning the king of Assyria. He shall not come near this city, nor shoot an arrow at it, nor come before it with a shield, nor cast up siegeworks against it. He shall return by the same way he came, without entering the city, says the LORD. I will shield and save this city, for my own sake, and for the sake of my servant David.

Isaiah 37:21-35

I turned to the Lord God, pleading in earnest prayer, with fasting, sackcloth, and ashes. I prayed to the Lord, my God, and confessed, "Ah, Lord, great and awesome God, you who keep your merciful covenant toward those who love you and observe your commandments! We have sinned, been wicked and done evil;; we have rebelled and departed from your commandments and your laws. We have not obeyed your servants the prophets, who spoke in your name to our kings, our princes, our fathers, and all the people of the land. Justice, O Lord, is on your side; we are shamefaced even to this day: the men of Judah, the residents of Jerusalem, and all Israel, near and far, in all the countries which you have scattered them because of their treachery towards you. O LORD, we are shamefaced, like our kings, our princes, and our fathers, for having sinned against you. But yours, O Lord, our God, are compassion and forgiveness! Yet we rebelled against you and paid no heed to your command, O LORD, our God, to live by the law you gave us through your servants the prophets. Because all Israel transgressed your law and went astray, not heeding your voice, the sworn malediction, recorded in the law of Moses, the servant of God, was poured out over us for our sins. You carried out the threats you spoke against us and against those who governed us, by bringing upon us in Jerusalem the greatest calamity that has ever occurred under heaven. As it is written in the law of Moses, this calamity came full upon us. As we did not appease the LORD, our God, by turning back from our wickedness and recognizing his constancy, so the LORD kept watch over the calamity and brought it upon us. You, O LORD, our God, are just in all that you have done, for we did not listen to your voice.

"Now, O Lord, our God, who led your people out of the land of Egypt with a strong hand, and made a name for yourself even to this day, we have sinned, we are guilty. O Lord, in keeping with all your just deeds, let your anger and your wrath be turned away from your city Jerusalem, your holy mountain. On account of our sins and the crimes of our fathers, Jerusalem and your people have become the reproach of all our neighbors. Hear, therefore, O God, the prayer and petition of your servant; and for your own sake, O Lord, the your face shine upon your desolate sanctuary. Give ear, O my God, and listen; open your eyes and see our ruins and the city which bears your name. When we present our petition before you, we rely not on our just deeds, but on your great mercy. O Lord, hear! O Lord pardon! O Lord be attentive, and act without delay, for your own sake, O my God, because this city and your people bear your name!"

I was still occupied with my prayer, confessing my sin, and the sin of my people Israel, presenting my petition to the LORD, my God, on behalf of his holy mountain---I was still occupied with this prayer, when Gabriel, the one whom I had seen before in vision, came to me in rapid flight at the time of the evening sacrifice.

Daniel 9:3-21

But then a hand touched me, raising me to my hands and knees. "Daniel, beloved," he said to me, "understand the words which I am speaking to you; stand up, for my mission now is to you." When he said this to me I stood up trembling. "fear not, Daniel," he continued; "from the first day you made up your mind to acquire understanding and humble yourself before God, your prayer was heard>"

Daniel 10:10-12

But susanna cried aloud:"O eternal God, you know what is hidden and are aware of all things before they come to be: you know that they have testified falsely against me. Here I am about to die, though I have done none of the things with which these wicked men have charged me." The Lord heard her prayer. As she was being led to execution, God stirred up the holy spirit of a young boy named Daniel, and he cried aloud: "I will have no part in the death of this woman."

Daniel 13:42-46

"Ask and it will be given to you; seek and you will find; knock and the door will be opened to you. For everyone who asks, receives, and the one who seeks, finds; and the one who knocks the door will be opened. Which one of you would hand his son a stone when he asks for a loaf of bread, or a snake when he asks for a fish? If you then, who are wicked, know how to give good gifts to your children, how much more will your heavenly Father give good things to those who ask him.

Matthew7:&-11

They walked about in the flames, singing to God and blessing the Lord. In the fire Azariah stood up and prayed aloud: "Blessed are you, and praiseworthy, O Lord, the God of our fathers, and glorious forever is your name. For you are just in all you have done; all your deeds are faultless, all your ways right, and all your judgments proper. You have executed proper judgments in all that you have brought upon us and upon Jerusalem, the holy city of our fathers. By a proper judgment you have done all this because of our sins; For we have sinned and transgressed by departing from you, and we have done every kind of evil. Your commandments we have not heeded or observed, nor have we done as you ordered us for our good. Therefore all you have brought upon us, all you have done to us, you have done by a proper judgement. You have handed us over to our enemies, lawless and hateful rebels; to an unjust king, the worst in all the world. Now we cannot open our mouths; we, your servants who revere you, have become a shame and a reproach. For your name's sake, do not deliver us up forever, or make void your covenant. Do not take away your mercy from us, for the sake of Abraham, your beloved, Isaac your servant, and Israel your holy one, To whom you promised to multiply their offspring like the stars of heaven, or the sand on the shore of the sea. For we are reduced, O Lord, beyond any other nation brought low everywhere in the world because of our sins. We have in our day no prince, prophet or leader, no holocaust, sacrifice, oblation, or incense, no place to offer first fruits, to find favor with you. But with contrite heart and humble spirit let us be received; As though it were holocausts of rams and bullocks, or thousands of fat lambs, SO let our sacrifice be in your presence today as we follow you unreservedly; for those who trust in you cannot be put to shame. And now we follow you with our whole heart, and fear you and we pray to you. Do not let us be put to shame, but deal with us in your kindness and great mercy. Deliver us by your wonders, and bring glory to your name, O Lord: Let all those be routed who inflict evils on your servants; Let them be shamed and powerless, and their strength broken; Let them know that you alone are the Lord God, glorious over the whole world."

Daniel 3:24-45

Then, when the whole assembly of the people was praying outside at the hour of the incense offering, the angel of the Lord appeared to him, standing at the right of the altar of incense. Zechariah was troubled by what he saw, and fear came upon him. But the angel said to him, "Do not be afraid Zechariah, because your prayer has been heard. Your wife Elizabeth will bear you a son, and you shall name him John.

Luke 1:10-13

And he said to them, "Suppose one of you has a friend to whom he goes at midnight and says, 'Friend, lend me three loaves of bread, for a friend of mine has arrived at my house from a journey and I have nothing to offer him,' and he said in reply from within, 'Do not bother me; the door has already been locked and my children and I are already in bed. I cannot get up to give you anything.' I tell you, if he does not get up to give him the loaves because of their friendship, he will get up to give him whatever he needs because of his persistence.

Luke 11:5-8

"And I tell you, ask and you will receive; seek and you will find; knock and the door will be opened to you. For everyone who asks, receives; and the one who seeks finds; and to the one who knocks, the door will be opened. What father among you would hand his son a snake when he asks for a fish? Or hand him a scorpion when he asks for an egg? If you then, who are wicked, know how to give good gifts to your children, how much more will the Father in heaven give the holy Spirit to those who ask him?"

Luke 11:9-13

"Simon, Simon, behold Satan has demanded to sift all of you like wheat, but I have prayed that your own faith may not fail; and once you have turned back, you must strengthen your brothers."

Luke 22:31-32

Then going out he went, as was his custom, to the Mount of Olives, and the disciples followed him. When he arrived at the place he said to them, "Pray that you might not undergo the test." After withdrawing about a stone's throw from them and kneeling, he prayed, saying, "Father, if you are willing, take this cup away from me; still, not my will but yours be done." [And to strengthen him an angel from heaven appeared to him. He was in such agony and prayed so fervently that his sweat became like drops of blood falling on the ground.] When he rose from prayer and returned to his disciples, he found them sleeping from grief. He said to them, "Why are you sleeping? Get up and pray that you may not undergo the test."

Luke 22:39-46

Their message was: "We send you funds, with which you are to procure holocausts, sin offerings, and frankincense, and to prepare cereal offerings; offer these on the altar of the LORD our God, and pray for the life of Nebuchadnezzar, king of Babylon, and that of Belshazzar, his son, that their lifetimes may equal the duration of the heavens above the earth; and that the LORD may give us strength, and light to our eyes, that we may live under the protective shadow of Nebuchadnezzar, king of Babylon, and that of Belshazzar, his son, and serve them long, finding favor in their sight. Pray for us also to the LORD, our God; for we have sinned against the LORD, our God, and the wrath and anger of the LORD have not been withdrawn from us at the present day.

Baruch 1:10-13

After giving the deed of purchase to Baruch, son of Neriah, I prayed thus to the LORD: Ah, Lord God, you have made heaven and earth by your great might, with your outstretched arm; nothing is impossible to you. You continue your kindness through a thousand generations; and you repay the father's guilt even to the lap of their sons who follow them. O God, great and mighty, whose name is the LORD of hosts, great in counsel, mighty in deed, whose eyes are open to all the ways of men, giving to each according to his ways, according to the fruit of his deeds: you have wrought signs and wonders in the land of Egypt and to this day, both in Israel and among all other men, until now you have gained renown. With strong hand and outstretched arm you brought your people Israel out of the land of Egypt amid signs and wonders and great terror. This land you gave them, as you promised their fathers under oath, a land flowing with milk and honey. They entered and took possession of it, but they did not listen to your voice; by your law they did not live, and what you commanded they failed to do. Hence you let all these evils befall them. See, the siegeworks have arrived at this city to breach it; the city will be handed over to the Chaldeans who are attacking it, amid sword, famine, and pestilence. What you threatened has happened, you see it yourself; and yet you tell me, O LORD GOD: Buy the field with money, call in witnesses. But the city has already been handed over to the Chaldeans.

Jerimiah 32:16-25

www.ingramcontent.com/pod-product-compliance
Lightning Source LLC
Chambersburg PA
CBHW061339140726
47997CB00003B/1020